The Pipe

Poetry of Recovery

Russell Pelletier

authorHOUSE®

AuthorHouse™
1663 Liberty Drive
Bloomington, IN 47403
www.authorhouse.com
Phone: 1 (800) 839-8640

Published by AuthorHouse   03/19/2016

ISBN: 978-1-5049-8658-8 (sc)
ISBN: 978-1-5049-8656-4 (hc)
ISBN: 978-1-5049-8657-1 (e)

Print information available on the last page.

This book is printed on acid-free paper.

Contents

For Your Enjoyment

Forward

This book is dedicated to all the people seeking recovery from addiction, and to those who live with and are friends of them. Good luck, good health, God bless.

Acknowledgement

This book was only possible because of the support of my wife Nancy, my best friend, Alice, and Sonny, a family member, whose computer skills brought the project together.

The Pipe

When I say things that people like,
I find it very odd,
that people give me credit for
what belongs to God.
God is the author of all I say,
I just pass the word along.
For me to take the credit would
be arrogant and wrong.
Let others pat their own backs.
I am not the type.
I know His words are the water
and I am just the pipe.
I'm thankful for the gift I'm given,
but I'm always quite aware.
I know who gave it to me
and who put it there.

I wrote The Pipe at Wegman's one night after I told someone
what I do is a gift, I didn't earn it. I am just the conduit.

The Cracked Glass

Is the glass half empty, or half
full, we are often asked.
It's not that simple in my case,
although I wish it were.
I fill my glass with thoughts of good, but it
doesn't stay that way. My glass is cracked
and must be filled, each and every day.
Just like my glass my life does
not stay filled each day.
I have to use my mind to fill my glass
with good. That's the way to view
my life, and realize the good.
So I do my part and decide
which answer's true.
The crack is not a bad thing, it
makes me work to fill it. Then I can
have some Joy, If I only will it.

About perspective, and what it takes to keep it healthy.

Free Advice

They say the best things in life are
free, but that's not always reality.
We must never forget, free advice
is worth what you pay for it.
We are so generous with our thoughts, but
one shoe doesn't fit you and your brother.
What's right for one is not for another.
When I know what's for you, there
is one thing I know is true. When
I take advice down off the shelf I
should really keep it to myself.

This is about the value of free advice, given or taken.

It's All Good

When things don't go like I think they
should; I must remember; it's all good.
When we accept its all god's plan,
we're free to do the best we can.
So now when I think 'This can't be good',
I know things happen as they should.
No need to thrash ourselves with doubt.
In the end, it will all work out.

About knowing every occurrence is God's will.

Ripples

We never know how far it goes
when we touch a life.
The ripples that travel from the
splash of a heartfelt deed traverse
not just distance but time as well.
It's sometimes many years before
the good shines back on you.
When, after a long time, someone says
"You helped me once and changed
my life" the ripples wash back over
you and fill you with wonder.
Sometimes it's just a small thing, but
the ripples of time can make it large.

Inspired by a friend, who did not know the
effect of her compassion and friendship.

The Sparrow

The sparrow lives just for today.
Not tomorrow or yesterday.
He searches for his food and mate,
and leaves the rest all up to fate.
He doesn't try to guess what's next.
He only tries to live his best.
Perhaps the sparrow is smarter than I.
He never needs to wonder why.
I could learn from a tiny bird,
who never utters a single word.

Living in today.

Islands Are Lonely

When you choose to be alone,
because you're in a slump.
And shut out your Higher Power
because you feel it cannot help.
It makes the black hole deeper
and harder to escape.
The way out isn't easy, someone
has to make the first move.
Courage is what it takes to change,
but it's a simple thing.
No one knows our wants and needs
if we don't say something.

About isolation.

Pages

I write about the things I feel
and sometimes what I see.
It helps me live my life anew,
and helps my sanity.
What I can't say I can write,
I do not hear the page.
Nor is it afraid of me, my fear, and rage.
My fears and woes don't loom so large,
when I write them down.
The thoughts that leave my pen are clear,
no longer harmful now.

This is about the power of journaling to reduce fear.

Feelings

Who teaches us not to be us?
Where do we learn not to feel,
or say what we feel?
You don't really feel that way do you?
Good little girls don't get angry.
Strong little boys don't cry.
Good Christians don't have
those kind of feelings.
Yes they do and we do too.
God gives us feelings to feel and
the right to say what we feel.
I'll take his word about it, not theirs,
and be grateful to feel what I feel.

About how we learn to feel, and who teaches us.

Balance

We start too slow, then go too fast.
At such a pace we cannot last.
We do too little, then too much.
We seem to lack the even touch.
We cling too hard and then discard
the things that matter most.
We cannot walk the tightrope
of life without balance.

This is about staying centered.

The Truth of My Strength

The truth of my strength is hard to see.
Most don't see it goes beyond me.
I have a look of outward strength
that people think is real.
The inner strength is where it's at
and that's the real deal.
I have no need to fear and fret
because of what's not happened yet.
I'll handle things when they arrive
and just be thankful I'm alive.
The truth of where my strength comes from
is no deep mystery.
My Higher Power fuels my faith.
That's good enough for me.

This is about where my strength really comes from.

The Bumble Bee of Chaos

There is a bumble bee that
buzzes through our heads.
It tells us we must do something
and fills our heart with dread.
If we listen to its buzz we get
all wound up tight.
Then it doesn't matter if it's
wrong or if it's right.
But if we wait, and keep our
faith the buzzing goes away.
Then the bumble bee of chaos
gives up and goes away.

This is about waiting chaos out, instead of fighting it.

The Road to Recovery

I walked down a road I didn't know,
to see where it would go.
It stretched before me like a
large sinewy snake.
Along the way I learned of life
and many wondrous things.
It seemed to me I needed more,
so I walked a little further.
I never turned back to where I was.
I saw no reason too.
I found the road has no end
but I saw on it a sign.
No surprise to me I thought,
RECOVERY was its name.

This is about how recovery leads us to good health.

The Hidden Things

What we hide keeps us apart.
Then we cannot speak our heart.
The hidden thing is never good.
We cannot be open, as we should.
When we dodge the thing we fear,
the truth is lost, we cannot hear.
When we say the things we feel,
It makes life special and very real.
The hidden things should be brought out,
to take away the fear and doubt.

This was an assignment from my teacher
and mentor, Lorraine, who told me to write
about secrets, without using the word.

Time

Once time is spent it won't return.
There's not a lot of it to burn.
Being idle is okay, if it's what you
choose today. So go fishing, or work in
the yard. Using it well is not so hard.
Just remember, it may be free,
but it doesn't go on endlessly.
Time is not an endless well, so keep
it precious and use it well.

About the importance of time.

It's Only a Mistake

I feared the words.
I feared the effect.
I feared the shame.
Then I learned the good.
I saw the lesson.
I found the worth.
A thing is just a thing.
What I do with it matters most.
Now I don't fear the words.
I don't fear the effect.
I don't feel the shame.
I can say it now and learn from it.
I made a mistake.
About how admitting a
mistake can be good.

To Have What They Have

I see people fruitful and happy and
I would like to be that way.
Could it happen? I often wonder.
Do I have what it takes to
have what others have?
There is one answer to the questions.
A simple one I can use.
If I want what others have, I
must do what they do.

What I must do to get the happiness others have.

God Drives the Bus

I do my best, God does the rest,
to get the things I need.
I know the things I want, but
not what's best for me.
It's good that I don't drive the bus,
I don't know where I'd go.
It's better that I take the ride
with one who's in the know.
I can decide and be all wrong,
it matter not a bit.
If God doesn't like my choice, he
has the power to change it.
I have no need to fear my choice,
if I listen, and hear His voice.

This verse was inspired by my friend, Clyde,
who uses this metaphor a lot, and by my Mentor,
Tommy, who always says "God is going to get what
he wants. It means we need not fear decisions.

Lean On Me

God sends me people when I need them.
Each new one helps me in a different way
and through a separate time.
It's alright to lean on them for a while,
if I don't push them down.
The idea is to draw strength from these
friendships without draining the friend.
Balance is the key.
Go figure.
Each new friend and friendship makes me
stronger, happier, more complete.
What an awesome gift.

This is about counting on your friends
without sucking the life out of them.

The Path

There is a path to faith that doesn't
follow the long dusty road of doubt.
It winds not its way through the
valley of self-pity or the forest of
blame and ridicule.
The way to faith travels along the
sunlit trail of affirmation and trust.
Upon coming to the bridge of reason,
it crosses to the shore of faith
and the love of our Higher Power.

The way to faith.

The Struggle

If I could climb every hill
and not wear down,
cure every ill in every town,
win every fight with courage and might,
never be wrong and always be right,
How could I ever grow any stronger,
with nothing to strive for any longer,
It's not results that make us strong,
but how we struggle to get along.
It's more about the road I choose,
not if I win or if I lose.
For if I give God my very best,
I'll always be so very blessed.

The journey is what matters.

A Lesson

Sometimes I learn from
the loud or the dull.
It seems they all have something.
I never know how it will come.
It's always God's surprise.
Once I listened to someone
I didn't want to hear,
and he told his simple way to learn.
He said, you people lead with your
heart and I follow with mine.

How we can learn from anyone.

Steps

He took the first step, then the rest.
His way was slow, he did his best.
Through years of work he
stretched and grew.
It changed his life and made it new.
He passed it on as best he could.
He came to see that it's all good.
Now he looks to life ahead,
without the worry and the dread.
His Higher Power leads him on,
to the promise of a bright new dawn.

The benefit of the steps.

Emerging

He seemed so sad for one so young,
when he spoke of all the things he'd done.
The path he chose had made him strong.
He learned who he was, all along.
Now his life is full and bright,
no longer one long endless night.
His story gives us all great joy.
Now a young man, no more a boy.

This poem is about David, who spoke at the Holiday
Weekend Getaway. He was eighteen and emerging.

The Mirror

I met a man I didn't like, though
I did not know him well.
I'll never like this guy, I thought.
I came to know him more and
more and then I got the point.
He's just like me, I realized,
how could I be to him?
I couldn't be a friend to me it
seemed, so how could I to him?
I had to learn to like us both.
I don't need to fear the mirror, now.
I like what I see there.
The man and I became good friends
when I learned to like us both.

This is about how we see in others what
we don't like in ourselves, and how we can
become friends with almost anyone.

Shake It Off

What can I do when a problem comes?
Shake it off.
When people test me, what's the way?
Shake it off.
How do I face challenge and controversy?
Shake it off.
How do I make an ending
into a beginning?
Shake it off.
I know God won't bury me
with the shovel of failure.
I can beat it all, if I can shake it off.

From the story of the mule in the well. Shake it off. Step up.

Catch Up Mode

We're always in the catch up mode.
There's always one behind.
One gives more than the other
and never seems to mind.
It seems it's never equal, for
two who really care.
I guess it doesn't have to be the
friendship is still there.
If we give up keeping score
and care all that we can
we all end up as winners and
no one is better than.
Catch up mode has too much stress
and blocks our way to happiness.

How one person in a relationship always cares more?

The Search

I do the things I think I can't
and wonder how.
I face the things I fear and whisper, wow.
I hear "That's great, what you can
do", and I ponder; could it be true?
The question remains unanswered.
Who am I? What am I? Where
do the gifts come from?
The search goes on and hope comes slowly,
as I try to feel special, not so lowly.
My blessings are legion, and I know it.
Someday I'll let the goodness in and
know how special life has been.

The search for the answer to the age old question, who am I?

The Committee

The committee, that does no good,
has an office in my head.
They spend their sessions
on gloom and dread.
Why do I let them live rent free
where they don't belong,
instead of fighting to be strong.
I have decided to chair the board
and be first on the list.
It's time to tell them they're dismissed.
There is one thing that I have learned.
They stay and stay if not adjourned.

What isolation and self doubt produce?

Comfort Zone

I find myself where I don't fit
and I lose some of my worth.
It doesn't have to be that way.
I can stay where I belong.
I don't have to measure up.
I can find where I fit in.
I need to let the others go.
They are not for me.
There are many I can feel at home
with, who don't need to measure me.
I will seek them out and make a
life of comfort and happiness.

Some social encounters I'm not well suited for.
They make me uncomfortable. I can leave.

Equals

When we let each other in, the walls
between our worlds grow thin.
The times when status matters
not and titles have no meaning,
make us see the truth of us and
change our lives with feeling.
This gift is ours for one another, and
makes us equals like no other.
While we hurtle through our
lives and fill our busy days,
we separate ourselves in oh so many ways.
But we can make the journey back,
to where we value all the same.
For life is a valued journey,
not a silly game.

Being equal serves us both.

Surrender

Is surrender a loss? It depends
on who is surrendered to.
Submission to a boss, a spouse
or a bully may be a loss.
Giving up the right to be
yourself serves no good.
If I surrender to my Higher Power and
keep my ego in check, it is a victory.
When I know God gets what he
wants, and all I can do is my part, I
win, God wins, everybody wins.
Control, manipulation, intimidation
and fear are not tools of recovery.
Surrender to my Higher Power and
acceptance of my place in the universe
is like an entire tool box for life.

Submission is not a good thing. Surrender can be.

The Raft of Recovery

I floundered in the River of Fear and
drifted to the Sea of Uncertainty.
I struggled to keep from drowning
for oh so many years.
My mind grew numb from trying
not to feel the truth of life.
I thought I wouldn't make it and
I nearly gave up the fight.
Then one day while thrashing
wildly to stay afloat,
I blundered onto the raft of recovery.
Here I found a place to rest, and
a chance to gain my strength.
Now I ride the raft in peace and
serenity and sometimes,
if I am lucky, I pull someone up with me.

A place of rest and refuge.

The Slap That Doesn't Sting

It used to all be personal.
I took it all to heart.
Now I know the truth of things
and I can see my part.
Some things people do have
nothing to do with me.
And those that do no longer
have to be so hard on me.
So now I know I'm not the
center of everything.
I find I'm able to take the
slap that doesn't sting.
The only one who can hurt me is me.

Only I can hurt me.

Favor

Why do we put limits on God?
I find such an act very odd.
A life of blessings has taught me well.
What God will give I can never tell.
God uses his pallet to color
the fabric of my life.
I need not see a limit.
My life will fill with endless
favor, if I let him in it.
It isn't wrong to expect the best.
I do what I'm able. God does the rest.

About the promise and blessing of God's favor.

The Cost of Anger

I know the price of gasoline and
bread, I buy them every day.
If they have a price tag I
know how much to pay.
The cost for these is simple and
cause me no dismay.
There is a thing that I pay for
that costs me rather steeply.
It does no good and wounds us all
with cuts that go quite deeply.
The costs are high in friends and
joy fills our lives with rancor.
Who can truly tell me then,
what is the cost of anger.

What does anger cost us?

The Way of the Hawk

She darts in and out of the trees,
like a great feathered butterfly.
At just the right moment she slashes
forward with her talons to end the
chase, but she misses her prey.
More often than not this is nature's result.
She does not chide herself or put
herself down because she missed.
She simply readies herself for the next time.
Is the Hawk wiser than we?

Animals don't fret about mistakes and failures.
Only humans pay for a mistake more than once.

Once Upon a Time

Once upon a time he thought he was tough.
He thought being numb
meant he was strong.
He thought no one could hurt him.
Once upon a time.
If he let no one in no one could hurt him.
That was how he lived his life.
Once upon a time.
Then he came to learn to feel and
he knew it was all wrong.
Now he loves and lives and cares
and feels the things he should.
He has the life he wished he had.
Once upon a time.

Being numb is not being tough.

A Hole in the Water

I put my hand in a bucket of water.
I pull it out the hole is gone.
I wish my heart was a bucket of water.
There's a hole in my heart I've never
filled. I'm told no one can fill it but me.
Not good news.
I work to make me happy and
perhaps be whole one day.
I try to learn the tools I need
and how to work with them.
If it's working I do not know,
and yet I can't give up.
I wish my heart was a bucket of water.

About feeling incomplete.

39

I Just Can't Help Myself

When I know I shouldn't
speak I do it anyway.
It doesn't matter if I'm right,
I have something to say.
I know I've done this many times.
I just keep coming back.
When it comes to piping up I
really have the knack.
People ask me why I can't leave
my opinion on the shelf.
I simply shrug my shoulders and
say "I just can't help myself".

When I should not speak, but I do, what happens.

The Time is Always Right

God wants us to flourish and
use the gifts He gave us.
It matters not how old we are
when we reach our peak,
Six or sixty he wants our best.
So don't hold back when you want to try.
When a dream appears it's never too late.
God's expectations have no expiration date.

There is no expiration date on God's gifts. It's never too late.

Instructions

Why would I think I'll get what I
want by giving God instructions?
Somehow He doesn't read the script I
had in my mind.
Why I think to bargain with the one who
holds the cards only makes sense to me.
Still, I try to bargain for what I think I
want, and wonder why it takes so long.
It never fails that when I wait and
try to be accepting, the outcome
is better than my plan.
So I'll try to wait for the good
in life and remember,
Why should God follow my
instructions? Nobody else does.

How foolhardy is it to tell God what to do?

Table for One

*If you want to be alone and miss
out on the fun, don't dine with
companions, get a table for one.
Bitterness should not be shared,
but friendship is a feast.
Never give up on the most,
or settle for the least.
Dessert you share is oh so sweet
and brings a smile to your face.
And sharing with your friends
makes the world a happy place.
So when the waiter asks how
many? never say table for one.
Set the table for your friends
and be the happy one.*

It's not all about Russ.

No One Ever Returned

They went across the bridge,
and no one ever returned.
They left behind a house of sorrow,
and no one ever returned.
The wagon of envy came unhitched,
and no one ever returned.
They stared down the face of fear,
and no one ever returned.
They found a place of peace,
and no one ever returned.

About how people don't usually change back.

Thank You for Right Now

*I can't control the future. I really don't
know how. The best that I can do is
say," Thank you for right now."
Most times the present is not a place
to fear. I can be quite happy if I just
remain right here. I think I know my
wants and needs and the way that
things should go. I need to be more
patient with the one who's in the know.
Now I look around and
sometimes just say" Wow!"
I need to keep remembering to
thank you for right now.*

About enjoying the moment.

Guilt Trip

*Pack your bags. We're going on a
trip. It's a ride we all know well.
Why we go so often, it's really hard to
tell. No one seems to like this trip, or
ever ask to go. Still we always get on
board, even though we dread it so.
The need to beat ourselves with the
club of self-abuse is powerful, and
deadly, though it has no real use.
So I think it's time for a different
trip to a sweeter kind of place. The
road to guilt won't serve my needs
or put a smile on my face.
Now when the train of guilt pulls
out I think I'll stay behind. It's
time to buy a ticket for a
trip of a better kind.*

This is about how useless guilt is. Inspired by Dottie,

Nightmare

Is a nightmare really a nightmare if you're
wide awake, or is it something else?
I can escape a dream by waking.
Life is another matter.
Sometimes I try to get away by using
mindless chatter, but when I stop it's
all the same. The chatter doesn't
change the game.
The real world won't go away, no
matter how I cry and pray.
My eyes are open. I can see.
The truth is plain.
It's up to me.

We cannot escape reality.

Getting By

I met a friend who seemed a little gray.
How are you I asked.
Getting by he replied and went away.
I met a hobo down by the tracks.
I asked him the same.
Getting by, was all he said.
I saw a farmer in a field,
sweat upon his brow.
How goes it, I asked.
Getting by was his reply as
he went about his task.
I met a man with a red tipped cane.
Getting by I asked?
I'm better than good, he
shouted with a smile
and I wondered who was really blind.

This is about how we perceive our lives.

Growing

I see things time and time again,
they never look the same.
I read the same words many times,
they never sound the same.
The thing that changes every time
is how I view these things.
I grow and change with every day.
That makes it all brand new.
And so I gain much more each time,
hoping always hoping, to keep growing.

Letting Go

How long can sorrow be carried
before it stays forever?
Any other burden we would gladly
shed when it becomes too heavy.
What then, do you put in its place to
fill the hole where the sorrow dwelt?
Some go numb, others mean
to block it out somehow.
Others carry on, for this too shall pass,
and they seek happiness and life.
For every day is new, and we can
choose to make it better, it's up to us.

This is about releasing guilt, sorrow and regret. It
came from my forty plus years of guilt and regret.

Courage Knows Fear

Who is brave, and who is not?
What is a courageous act?
To forge ahead fearlessly takes no courage.
Courage is a child who turns
off his night light.
It's a person who speaks in public
while they want to get sick.
Being honest with the ones who can
hurt you is a courageous act.
To carry on in spite of fear is bravery.
Fear can save my life if it keeps
me from acting foolishly,
but I don't have to be paralyzed
for I am not alone.

What courage really is.

Listening

Do I listen when I hear?
Do I get what finds my ears?
If I'm thinking what to say
or planning my reply,
It's as though I am not present
and I really wonder why.
To listen I must care what's
said and who the sayer is,
not just what I want to say and
what my viewpoint is.
So when I'm not hearing I must
say, more than to be heard,
I need to listen.

Willing

To know is not enough.
I must be willing.
Knowledge is an unused tool,
if there is no action.
I must choose to do the hard things.
If I blink or stall, I gain no ground.
Sometimes it's not wisdom
that gets me there.
A plan is not enough.
I must be willing.02-28-09

Knowledge is not enough.

Own It

I'd not have done this if they
had not done that.
That kind of logic is so old hat.
What they do can't make you act. It's
all your choice, as a matter of fact.
When we own the things we do it shows
our strength, our word is true.
The good we do is stronger when we lead
our lives as honest men. It really is easier
in the if we don't have to make amends

About responsibility for our actions.

Scars

Life is a circle that can heal our
scars and make us whole.
When we become as children
it gives us back our soul.
We can take the pain of early days,
and turn it back in many ways.
To pass down love and learning to a
child heals the scars and leads the way
to make us new again someday.
And so we make the circle whole,
and heal the scars upon our soul.

About healing the scars of childhood.

Sleep On It

When I close my eyes on something
it doesn't seem so bad.
Some rest and a little prayer
can make me feel less sad.
This too shall pass is really true,
so there is something I can do.
I can close my eyes on trouble and
sleep the whole night through.

About how twenty-four hours and a night's sleep
can take a great deal of anxiety out of a thing.

Greet the Dawn
Like a Dog

I want to greet the dawn like a dog.
To see the sun come up with a joyous
wagging tail would be a gift I could take.
Puppies never say" Five more
minutes" when it's time to get up.
Dogs and children know, "This
is a day the lord has made."
They haven't learned to dread the dawn.
I can't be a child or a dog, but
I can learn to act like one.

Dogs and small children live in the moment, what a gift.

Dividends

If I take the poison of hate, who will die.
If I shine peace on you which you
don't receive, it shines back on me.
Who is hurt?
The well of good does not run dry.
We're given all we want to share.
So if we put out all we can, we'll
get back all of it and more.
It costs nothing, pays back
more than money can buy and
we are better than ever.
Surely it is the greatest bargain on
earth and the sale never ends.

This verse is modeled after the Bible, shining peace
on the homes of the reluctant and doubters.

Soaring

Do they love what they do?
Or is it just natural.
We watch them soar and think
it glorious and exhilarating.
Do they feel it too?
We can soar too, if we allow it.
If we let go of the past and future we can
reach incredible heights today, and feel the
rush of the wind of serenity on our face
as we reach greater and greater heights.
It is not only the hawk that can soar.
If we choose to, we can too.

This is about choices and limitations.

I'm Never Alone

I walked along a dusty road,
tired from the heavy load.
The burdens seemed too much to bear,
with no one else to help or care.
It felt like there would never be
an end to the pain and misery.
But there was always someone there,
someone to watch who really cared.
When I let my Higher Power in,
my worries and fears began to end.
Now I know I am not alone
and I never really was.

Walking with God.

The Getaway

Where do you go when you have no hope?
When you feel you're at the
end of your rope.
Where do you go when you
can't tell friends?
You go to where the hope never ends.
You learn to love those with no last names,
who care about you, all the same.
These strangers may not have degrees,
but they teach you how to
become happy and free.
There is no charge for all this help.
It's given to you gladly and when
you pass it to someone
you know the work is never done.
And the miracle goes on and on.

About the Holiday Getaway Weekend in New Market Va.

What is Real

What is real, what is not?
We often wonder, do we not?
How we see the things we see
is all our own reality.
The truth is sometimes hard to find.
Our fears can often make us blind.
The light of faith can help us through,
and give our hearts a truer view.
Then we can trust our eyes and ears,
and put away our foolish fears.
Sought with the heart and not the mind,
the truth is not so hard to find.

Faith can show us what is real.

Looking After Me

I do what I need, and then what
I want, to find serenity.
Everything in balance is
the key to harmony.
I can't enjoy the games I like
if my work's undone.
Nobody else can do it.
I have to be the one.
When I feed my spirit, my
body and my mind,
I can go to the playground of
life and not feel out of line.
So if I'm feeling out of sorts I
know what I must do.
I put my life in balance.
It always sees me through.

Taking care of mind body and spirit.

Stepping Stone

When I share what I've done before,
I feel a whole lot lighter.
When I put the past behind me,
the future seems much brighter.
I can change my future as I please,
and put my conscience quite at ease.
I can look upon the past,
I do not need to stare.
It should not stop my growth
or make me linger there.
I will not run down the things
I see in my rear view mirror.
The future's where I need to look
and keep my vision clear.
So when I say where I was wrong,
it helps me grow and move along.
At last I can get past regret
and focus on what's coming next

About the fifth step.

Scarecrow of Fear

Sometimes the thing that
scares me isn't real.
That still doesn't change the way I feel.
Fear is the same to me.
Where it comes from is no matter.
It still makes me mad as a hatter.
Sometimes I can see the truth
and still win out,
if I face it squarely I can lose the doubt.
Imagination is the scarecrow of fear.
It seems to be what it is not,
and has no real power.

This is about how fear feels the same, real
or imagined, but has no real power.

Don't Get Pulled In

When others are down and look
to you, don't get pulled in.
If a friend walks on their lower
lip, don't get pulled in.
We work too hard to let things go,
and move ahead with life.
Don't get pulled in.
Some choose to wallow and never grow.
Don't get pulled in.
If misery loves company, it
doesn't have to be yours.
Don't get pulled in.
Hold your ground, move
ahead, don't get pulled in.

About not letting others negativity affect us.

Projecting

I hear the thing that hasn't come.
The future makes my brain go numb.
The thing that looms so large and tall,
may not happen, after all.
And if it does, I can work it out.
I needn't crumble under doubt.
But if it doesn't come today
the fear wins, anyway.
I need to wait to see tomorrow,
instead of planning on pain and sorrow.

I wrote this at a meeting about fear.

Turn on the Light

When I was young and I felt scared
there was something I could do.
Turn on the light.
When I need something I can't find,
there's something I can do.
Turn on the light.
If friends need help to find their way,
there's something I can do.
Turn on the light.
The light of reason can hold off fears,
show the way and help me see.
I just need to turn on the light.

Shining the light of reason.

Acceptance

I cannot love slices of people,
for they are what they are.
I cannot take the world in
part, for it is what it is.
The truth of life and of the world is not
a meal to be eaten one bit at a time.
The will of God is the way of all the
universe and cannot be taken piecemeal.
The only way to know the true meaning
of the plan is through acceptance.
It must be taken as a whole,
the way it is meant to be,
and enjoyed as fully as any meal could.

Inspired by a line from the movie First
Knight "I cannot love people in slices.'

The Plan

Why try to make God kill me,
if I couldn't stand to live.
Did I think that I could fool him
into doing what I couldn't?
Tricking God would not have
been an easy thing to do.
I'm glad I failed, it's not for
me to say my time is up.
God has a plan and when it's
done that will be the time.
Who knows when that will be?
Who wants to know?
Not me.
I think I'll see what's next for me.

Living out God's plan.

Voice Mail

When the phone rings with that same
old message, you don't have to listen.
That old recording that says your
stupid doesn't hold the truth, so
there's something you can do.
When you hear the message of
doubt don't pick up the phone.
Let it go to voice mail.

When old negative tapes play, don't listen.

Too Much to Do

Did you call a friend today?
No? Too much to do?
Did you talk to God today?
No? Too much to do?
Did you walk the earth today
and revel in its beauty?
No? Too much to do?
Did you help someone with
less than you today?
No? Too much to do?
Did you hug someone today,
or give them a smile?
No? Too much to do?
Did you let the sun warm your face today?
No? Too much to do?
Sometimes we might want to let something
go, when there's too much to do.

About what really matters.

Keep Smiling

So you smiled at a person you
just happened to meet.
A random act, with no real plan, so
why'd you do it? Because you can.
Some folks find it hard to smile.
They need a little aid.
But when you help them out you see, their
day is truly made. It may not seem to
matter much or cost you any money.
But the boost you give a stranger
is truly sweet as honey.
The world can be a better place, so
keep that smile upon your face.

About what a smile can mean, even to a stranger.

The Puzzle

Life is a puzzle, it would seem. We search
for answers to every little thing.
Our need to know can make us
sad, even drive us a little mad.
But we don't need it all. We
have someone who does.
So when we search for answers we
shouldn't think it odd; the answers
that we seek can all be found in God.
We will learn all we need to know, when
the time is right, no real need to hurry.
The answers to the puzzle are already
there; so we don't need to worry.
It's all good.

Another assignment from my mentor, Lorraine. Its about
the need we seem to have to understand the puzzle of life.

The Gift

There once was a man who could not feel
and the world to him seemed so unreal.
He wondered why he had so much
and still he felt so out of touch.
There came a time when he made friends
And he came to learn so much from them.
They taught him how to do his part,
when they wrapped their hands
around his stone cold heart.

About how I was when I came into recovery.

A Single Blade of Grass

The tallest buildings in the world
cannot begin to compare.
Rocket science is child's play beside it.
A two hundred miles per hour
sports car pales in its glow.
People think the things they
make are wonders to behold.
The truth is that the wonders
came before all that.
The miracles that make the world
great are at our very feet.
Science cannot make just one, or create
the miracle of a single blade of grass.

Life of any kind is a far greater thing than man can make.

Reruns

I did a thing that didn't work
so I tried is several times.
God rang the bell to let me know,
but I never heard the chimes.
I knew my just had to work.
I knew I must be right.
It never did, even though I
tried with all my might.
If this is pure insanity I
have to say I'm guilty.
I'll need to find a different way,
one that works for me.
Reruns always end the same.

The insanity of doing the same thing
repeatedly, expecting different results.

How Much

How beautiful can one day be?
How far can the heart and the spirit swell
with wonder from one sunrise to the next?
I've had such days, but cannot say
I know the answer to how much.
To feel the swell of gratitude and
the wonder of self-knowledge is
a feeling beyond compare.
These days are rare.
They come and go, so I relish every one.
So, how beautiful can one day be?
I really couldn't say.
I'll take each one without regret and
trust things will get better yet.

About a day of true wonder and gratitude.

Oasis of Peace

We walk through the desert of life,
thirsty for the drink of serenity.
Life can be a dry and dusty wasteland
of fear and uncertainty.
When we take the hand of a
friend we do not walk alone.
If we let another help us we can cross
the dunes of doubt and despair and
find our way to the Oasis of Peace.

Friends can help us through anything.

A Piece of My Mind

Someone once upset me, so 1 gave
him a piece of my mind.
If someone disagrees with me I can
give them a piece of my mind.
If someone doesn't get my point
of view, what can I do? I can give
them a piece of my mind.
But if I give everyone a piece of
my mind, I may have none left.

I shouldn't give away what I need for myself.

The Eye of Envy

*To see the good without the eye of
envy opens up a world beauty.
To be happy for others and their
good fortune makes one richer.
The hand of favor follows the hand
of gratitude. All of us are blessed, but
all do not know. As we see more we
garner more favor and blessings.
We can have it all through gratitude
if the eye of envy remains closed.*

Happiness for others good fortune comes back to us.

The Spoken Heart

Why refuse to speak your heart?
Why refuse to even start?
When you say what you should say
vanity and pride can't block the way.
When you say" They know how I feel"
that's not honest, not being real.
The love you give with the spoken word
cannot be shown with thoughts unheard.
What you mean and what you feel should
never go unspoken Silence cannot right
a wrong or make a heart unbroken.
Feel it, mean it, say, it, while you can.

We should speak our feelings before it's too late.
Once someone is gone it's too late.

The Chain

There is a chain we cannot see, that
holds us prisoner endlessly.
We pass it on, from father to son.
It seems its work is never done.
It passes pain down through the years
and isn't bothered by sorrow or tears.
Its strength is legend, with a
hold that's fierce. The links are
strong and hard to pierce.
Addiction can be broken though,
with another force unseen.
Faith is what can break it,
and bring us harmony.
There is a truth so very plain.
You and I can break the chain.

About breaking the generational chain
of addiction and its effects.

Do Something

When I am frozen, locked in fear
not feeling strong, I need to do
something, even if it's wrong.
God can change it, should he choose,
so I really have nothing to lose.
He always gets what he wants.
I knew it all along. I need to do
something, even if it's wrong.
God wants me to do my part. I just
need to follow my heart. I don't need to
know if I'm right or wrong. I just need
to do something, even if it's wrong

From the old saying, Do something if it's wrong.

Coasting

Sometimes it's hard to move ahead.
I'd much rather coast instead.
The work seems tough and never ending.
It feels like rules, stiff, and never bending.
New habits and routines
sometimes cause me fear.
That's when I'd sooner hide right here.
Moving ahead is not easy and still,
the only way to coast is downhill.

Growing versus coasting. The only way to coast is downhill.

Desperately Busy

There is a thing we do when fear makes
us dizzy. We block the thoughts of woe
when we become desperately busy.
Going hard without a break
gives us little time to think and
help us to avoid the brink.
Still there comes a time when
busy is not enough. In the end
we all must face our stuff.
When we've had all we can take we
need to give ourselves a break
No amount of activity will
ever be what sets us free.
We need to stop and face the test, do
our best, then let God do the rest.

What people do to avoid their feelings.

I'll Play These

I sat in the poker game of my life
and looked sadly at my hand.
I got nothing, I thought, no
place to take a stand.
I need some new cards, I said to God,
and thought that action very odd.
But when I asked my hand was redealt,
and it really changed the way I felt.
Now I play the game at ease. I look at
my hand and say "I'll play these."
Thank you Lord.

Inspired by Robyn, who looked at the hand of her life,
and thought, I'll play these.

Lamp of Faith

I wouldn't carry a lamp out in the
sunlight, or take a flashlight to lunch.
No need for light if it isn't dark.
God put his light in the dark places.
Perhaps we should, as well.
When we find ourselves in the dark places
we can use our faith to light our way.

Inspired by God putting his light, Jesus, in the dark places.

What Would I Change

What would I change if I could
turn back the years? Back to the
days when I knew no fears.
Would I take out the hurt and the
worries of life? Would I have only
joy and never know strife?
Maybe I would. It all sounds so
good. But God has a plan, and He
put me in it. I think I'd be wrong
to change a single minute. All the
failures, successes, pain, and joy have
molded me, both man and boy.
So what are the things I should
change if I could? It all came
from God. It must be all good.
So I wouldn't change a thing, even I could.

This is about everything in our past, good
or bad, makes us who we are today.

Blessings in Disguise

What about the special things
that I did not expect?
Sometimes the best things
are truly indirect.
What I don't see coming can be a
sweet surprise, so much than we
could see, right before our eyes.
We go for a walk and see a thing we
never thought we would. Then we smile
to ourselves and say, "Well it's all good."
Now when I have too much to do and
think I'm so hard pressed, I need to be
more grateful and realize I'm blessed.
I could have nothing much to
do, and little to do it with.
Being busy shows how much I'm blessed,
no need for me to feel distress.

If I did not have such wonderful blessings
to take care of would I be better off?

Good Enough

We always strive to be good enough. We try to measure up to other people's stuff. I know I'm good enough for God, so I find this behavior very odd. I wasn't put here to please you, but one thing I know is true. As long as I'm good enough for me, I don't have to be good enough for you.

About being good enough for me.

The Cherry Tree

When you're raised on bitter lemons and
turn sour naturally, it's hard to clean your
spirit with the fruit of the cherry tree.
We have a choice which fruit to
take It's up to us to pick it.
The sweeter is happier. The
cherry's just the ticket.
So where we were and who we
were is not what we have to be,
if we choose the cherry tree.
Each day we get to pick a tree.
It's up to us which it will be.
Happiness and hope is on the cherry tree.

About our choice of sweet or sour, in our life.

Goodbye Norman

Norman Rockwell is no more. We can't have what was before.
Times have changed and so have we.
We can love what we are today, and not compare with yesterday.
It's up to us to see the good, and love our lives as we all should. Life on a poster is nice to see, and it may draw a smile, but we can have it just as good, in a different time and style.

About the desire for a Rockwell like existence,
and how good things can be.

One Day

One day I'll do what I mean to do,
the things that I can treasure.
One day I'll make my dreams come
true, have joy beyond all measure.
One day my list will be all done. I'll
have the time for peace and fun.
If I can just get started, I'll do it
all, one day, if I take the time to
work, and put away the play.
Someday I'll find the perfect way,
and I won't have to say "One Day".

This is about the need to take care of business.

Lists

What do you do when you can't
keep track? What do you do when
you've lost your knack?
You make a list to stay in touch.
That way you don't lose so much.
A list can go most anywhere.
Lots go on the Frigidaire.
Bathroom mirrors hold them for you. The
visor of your car can hold them too.
When you get too many to control,
there is an answer to the clutter.
Tear them all up, and start another.

About compulsive list making.

Remember

Sometimes I think I've gone
nowhere, then I remember.
Sometimes I feel there's no better
way, then I remember.
Sometimes I think I'll never
matter, then I remember.
I remember where I started,
that cold lonely place.
I remember the new ways
and all of God's grace.
I remember the love on a dear friend's face.
That's when I know that it's all good,
and everything happens just as it should.
When I have worries, doubts or fears,
I remember, I remember.

About progress and where I started.

It's Never Too Late

They try so hard to show their dad
how much they've changed.
They've seen him grow and change
himself and they want him to know.
They have too.
It's said it's never too late and it's true.
If we can breathe we can change.
The same is true for them.
Hope is a powerful thing,
stronger than pride,
sweeter than arrogance,
clear as the mountain's air.

This is about people being able to change,
and that it is never too late.

The Garden of Fear

The head is a fertile garden.
Fear can blossom and flourish there.
Hidden in the dark recesses of the mind,
shielded from the light of truth,
it grows like a mushroom.
When the fear is spoken or written,
it returns to a smaller size
and loses its power.
Fear can be buried by the strength
of a power greater than us,
which can shine the light of
faith on a problem
and let us see it for what it really is.

This is about how easy fear can grow in the mind.

I'll Take the Good

I'll take the good and not ask why.
I must deserve to be so blessed
or else it wouldn't last.
But last it does and when it comes so fast
I can't understand it, I know.
I don't have to have the answers why.
The Giver knows the answer,
I just need to accept it and be grateful.
Sometimes answers aren't important.

It doesn't matter why I'm blessed, only that I am.

Good, Better, Best

I remember in the catalog there
was good, better, best
You could take what you
liked and leave the rest.
I try to lead my life today
in that very way.
I strive to choose the best of life,
every single day. So if the choice is
up to me, I'll choose the happiness.
In the catalog of life, I'll take not
good, not better, but best.

Inspired by my friend John's childhood experience.

In My Head

I stood upon the shore one night,
far from any distant light.
I thought of all the times I felt
like trying wasn't worth it.
I knew that it was in my head, and
there was nothing I should dread.
Why does it seem so hard to see
the wonders of reality?
The favor I have heaped on me seems
unreal, a thing I can't rely on.
I know the truth is that I can.
It's really up to me.
If I light the fire of reason the
truth is plain to see.

What I know versus what I feel.

I Knew It Was Coming

How often do we say it, I
knew it was coming?
To justify the gloom and we
see ourselves as seers.
Now the disappointment is not as
great, for knew of it's coming.
Why then don't we say it about
the good in our lives?
Maybe we just don't expect it.
I knew that hammer would hit my thumb,
but I never saw that check coming.
Maybe, with a change of heart
we can learn to say it of favor,
I knew it was coming!

If we expect the worst, it seems less
painful. Why not expect the best?

102

They Ain't Looking

Sometimes when I feel hurt,
I think, I'll show them.
My anger and my pain make me feel
I can show others by hurting them.
So I make my plan to show them
pain, but I fail to realize, "You can't
show em if they ain't lookin.

About I'll show them, and how it doesn't work.

If Only Things Were Different

If only things were different, then I'd
be alright. I'd never have to toss and
turn. I'd sleep right through the night.
More money, clothes and romance
would fix all of my woes.
If only things were different,
but that's the way it goes.
I ask the lord for what I want,
and He gives me what I need.
I also get direction, if only I'd take heed.
If only things were different
I'd be happy all the time.
The truth is, being happy
doesn't cost a dime.
So maybe it's the truth, of
how things ought to be.
The thing that should be different
is, quite simply, me.

The only thing we need to change is ourselves.

The Beauty of Ordinary Days

When I was young I searched for
fun in many exciting ways.
Now I find contentment in the
beauty of ordinary days.
The pleasure of the everyday
is often lost to youth.
What we take for granted
holds a satisfying truth.
A walk in the park or a game with
a dog may not seem to hold great
value, but to those can't enjoy them,
they're special things to do.
So when we sleep in comfort and shop
our well stocked stores, we can all be very
grateful we don't live on distant shores.
When we're feeling disappointed
about life's bumpy waves we
must remember the beauty
of ordinary days.

Gratitude for everyday blessings.

What Happened to Today

Sometimes I look too far ahead, and
fill my life with fear and dread.
The wreckage of the future is not mine to
fix. That power's not in my bag of tricks.
Today is the day I have to use.
Control of the future is just a ruse.
So I don't want to have say,
"What happened to today?"

People worry so much about yesterday and tomorrow that they forget about today, which is really all we have.

The Way of Light

In the darkest hour of night, when the
singer can't sing and the poet can't write,
the iron cage of doubt closes on your heart.
You long to set it free, but you
don't know where to start.
It matters not if it's real. It doesn't
change the way you feel.
The darkness doesn't know you. Everyone's
the same. Dread and sorrow are what
it brings. It only has one game.
Life is filled with many times when the
darkness pays a visit, and often times
we ask ourselves, "It isn't real, is it?"
Each time we come back to the light we
get a little stronger. The darkness doesn't
cage our heart, or hold us any longer.
This too shall pass, it's often said.
We need not live our lives in dread.
The way of light lies just ahead.

How everything makes us stronger, if we fight self-doubt.

Don't Sleep On Your Anger

As the sun goes down, remember
this, there's something you can do.
You cannot let the sun go down
with your anger still in you.
So let it go each day, before you try to sleep.
Then spend your night in quiet,
like the ones the shepherd keeps.
In dreams you can fix nothing.

It is not good to go to bed angry.

Is Silence Better Than a Lie?

Is it better to hold your tongue,
or tell a lie to spare someone?
The truth is best. We know it's true,
but if it hurts, what do you do?
Silence or omission can still be a lie.
Sometimes we want the easy way,
Which is right, it's hard to say?
In the end we will not lose, if we
let our conscience choose.

Is being silent to spare feelings better than telling a lie?

So Close

I could've missed it all.
I came so close.
I almost had no life.
I came so close.
I might have never seen the light.
I came so close.
I could have never known peace.
I came so close.
I nearly had no friends, family or God.
I came so close.
Too close.

The slender thread that pulled me into recovery.

The Time is Now

Say it now, no need to wait.
Before you blink it's just too late.
The perfect time and place may dawn,
after the one you love is gone.
You can say it now and every day.
There is no limit, don't delay.
To speak your heart will not grow old.
Give it away, it won't run out.
Never ever leave room for doubt.
When it's time for them to go,
you won't wonder, did they know.

Why I should say how I feel, and why I shouldn't wait.

Sanctuary

There is a place that has no
walls, yet it still protects us.
We come here in our pain and
learn that there is justice.
There are no ladders here.
The circle makes us equal.
When we need it, it's always there.
How odd to be where strangers care.
We learn to cope in this special place.
As times goes by a miracle occurs,
so slowly we don't notice.
We become a part of the
sanctuary that saved us.

About a place that has no material existence.
It lives in the mind and heart.

It Is What It Is

What is the meaning of a beautiful flower?
Why don't friends answer the phone?
Why does the sun never miss a day?
Why do people do what they do?
I search for that which doesn't have to be.
Sometimes a cigar is just a cigar.
Sometimes the meaning isn't hidden.
Sometimes it is what it is.
That's a good thing.

Everything doesn't analyze, or have a hidden meaning.

Back to Square One

When old behavior clouds my
mind, there is a place I go.
Back to Square One.
A slip turns back all the clocks.
Back to Square One.
When I shut my Higher Power
out I travel back in time.
Back to Square One.
When I think that I'm in charge,
I use the same old route.
Back to Square One.
Sometimes it doesn't hurt to
return to where it all began.
To move ahead sometimes I need to return,
Back to Square One.

Sometimes to move forward we need
to return to the beginning.

Silence – The Original

*Is silence a thing, or a lack of a thing,
at once a weapon and a defense?
How it is at once a relief and
a bitter crushing weight is an
amazing paradox of life.
Few indeed are the things that can
be used, endured or enjoyed.
If silence is really golden it
can be leaden as well.
Silence is truly one of God's
most amazing creations.*

What is silence?

It's Not Personal

The owl eats every other bird.
Is he bloodthirsty?
The bear gently tends her young.
Is she a gentle creature?
The ant and the bee are always working.
Are they diligent?
The trout is fooled by some
hair tied to a hook.
Is it gullible?
I think not.
They simply do what comes naturally.
How can I blame people
for doing the same.
It isn't always personal.

Not everything people do is personal.
Sometimes it is just what they do.

The Noose of Self Doubt

I wear a noose around my
neck. I put it there myself.
Only I can take it off, it's all in my control.
While I wear it I do not grow
or move the way I should.
It takes away my courage, and
blocks out all the good.
So if I choose to take it off
I can still win out.
Only I can set me free, from
the noose of doubt.

Self-doubt is from our own mind.

The Hand of Gratitude

Will I ever be happy groping for what
I want with the hand of envy?
If I resent what others have, I can't see my
blessings through the haze of resentment.
I pray to love what I have someday,
when I see through the haze of self-
pity, I can accept what God gives
me with the hand of gratitude.

Learning to love what I have.

If Only

If only I had tried harder.
If only.
If only I could change the past. If only.
If only people loved me more.
If only.
If only all the bad was good, and I did
not have to feel the pain. If only.
If only I were rich and healthy I
would have no need of fear.
If only.
If only cannot help me now.
Only faith can show me how.
Then I won't need "If Only".

About how all the excuses in the world
don't matter, only what we do.

For Your Enjoyment

*I have included some examples of my work
for you to enjoy during your recovery.*

That Sweet Old Dog

An old dog is the sweetest thing.
It loves you gently and gives
you all its heart.
He may not fetch or hunt anymore,
but you won't forget how he once did.
And when he's gone you'll always
feel the love of that sweet old dog.

Inspired by all my dogs.

Tubby the Bluegill

Tubby the bluegill was swimming
around one fine spring looking
for a little breakfast because that's
what bluegills do when he spotted
what looked like a big hat worm.
Tubby rushed over and grabbed
the worm quick as a cat, which
is pretty fast for a fish.
As soon as Tubby got the worm in his
mouth he knew it did not taste or feel
like any worm he had ever eaten.
Suddenly Tubby felt a sting in his
lip and he was pulled through the
water at a terrifying pace.
The next thing Tubby knew he was
lifted out of the water into the
open air, where he had never been.
That was when the hand of the
fisherman closed around him.
This is awful thought Tubby.
I'm in the skillet now.
Then the fisherman did an
unexpected thing.

He took the hook out of Tubby's
mouth and said "Thanks for giving
me so much fun" and he released
Tubby to fight again someday.
That same day the fisherman and his
son, whose name was Bradley, caught
Tubbys older and younger brothers Chubby
and Brawny and released them also.

When the fisherman and his son decided
to try a different bait they caught
Tubbys cousin, Chris the Crappie.
To his great surprise he was released also.
The fisherman and his son enjoyed
the day, very much, and decided they
would catch "lunch" another day.

My son and I made this up on a trip to the lake.

What Color is a Shadow

What color is a shadow?
Is it black? I think not.
He follows her every move, keeping
her in sight, for he no longer hears.
When she moves so does he.
His eyes eagerly follow her every
move in his waking hours.
His bed is always near her.
She takes his care much like a child
and he adores her the same way.
What color is a shadow?
It is the color of marsh grass, or a
big yellow dog named Biscuit.

This is about my wife and the big yellow dog.

The Last Pear

Once there were many.
Now there's but one.
What makes one the first to
go, then one the last?
The birds, the deer, and men
have all had their share.
What falls to the ground doesn't stay there.
So what makes the last, the last?
Perhaps it has hidden from the wind,
and gotten the sun just right.
Or maybe the fellow is closer to the
trunk and sweeter than the rest.
Who can say what makes a pear
the last one on the tree?
It matters not, for when he falls;
he'll be just like the rest.
None hold on forever, perhaps
he's just the best.

This was my first assignment from my mentor, Lorraine.

The Sweetest Dream

The sweetest dream I ever had
I never closed my eyes.
It lasted years and pulled me
through laughter, pain and tears.
Sometimes the dream seemed
unclear or painful to my heart.
I always knew you were the
one, I felt if from the start.
That dreams could last so many
years I never really knew.
And through it all I've been so
blessed, to once be loved, by you.

For my wife on Valentine's Day 2009.

The Blanket

It came without a sound last night, and
covered the earth in silky white.
To see the snow among the wood,
makes the world seem calm and good.
It blankets out the dull and dreary,
and our hearts feel much less weary.
Winter gives a special gift,
beauty in a pure white drift.
And when the children come to play,
spring seems not so far away.

Another assignment from Lorraine, to write about snow.

Mosquito Hawk

She moves like nothing else can.
One of the oldest there is on earth,
no need to change.
Like musical notes dancing across the page,
she hovers and darts about the marsh.
She hunts with beauty and grace
and seems to have no fear of me.
She lands on my arm with her
prey, perfectly at home.
She has her meal and watches me,
then she's gone.
Not a bug but a force of nature.
Dragonfly is perfect,
just how God made her.

Inspired by a dragonfly which had a
meal while sitting on my arm.

Beware the Moors

Beware the Scottish Moors at night.
What you find will cause you fright.
They say these things do not exist, but
who can say what prowls the mist?
Time means almost nothing there.
There's evil in the very air.
To those who move about the
dark, heed this final warning.
If you brave the moors at night
you will not see the morning.
But take heart and don't dismay.
The evil fears the light of day.

My first attempt at the eerie or surreal.

Daughter to the Stars

She winds like a silver ribbon through the
beauty of the valley that bears her name.
She has brought joy and sustenance
to so many for countless years.
Now, in her old age she is no less beautiful.
Her power to bring contentment
and happiness
still flows from her like her waters.
She is a jewel in the crown of nature
and her beauty is timeless.
She is Shenandoah, Daughter to the Stars.

The beauty of the Shenandoah River.

America's Monument

They look down on the place they built,
and the sight of it makes me wonder.
Would they stoop to help us now,
or simply plow it under?
The land that they envisioned
is surely different now.
It's gone so many different ways.
They'd surely wonder how.
But even though it's not the same,
it's still a place of purpose.
I'm sure they'd dig right in and
give their all to help us.
Mt. Rushmore is a symbol of
four great men, it's true.
But more, it is a symbol, of what
they did, for me and you.

About Mt. Rushmore, and how things have changed
since the monument was created.

Otter Games

I used to know an otter, but I
never knew his name.
He didn't know mine either but
he liked me just the same.
I'd go out on the water and
he would soon appear.
He seemed to like my presence
and he showed no real fear.
I would paddle and fish, and
he'd enjoy the day.
He seemed to tell me "Mister,
won't you come and play?"
I'd chase him for a while then
he'd leave me for behind.
He always came right back
again, as if he didn't mind.
We played this game for many
years, till he no longer came.
Now he's just a memory, but I
loved him just the same.

This is a true story about an otter at the
lake where I spend a lot of time.

Teach Your Children

We may not be aware but we
teach our children much.
Whether we intend to, it really matters not.
So how we teach and what we
teach is really ours to choose.
We give our children what they
need to help them win, or lose.
We cannot leave it up to chance, we
must make a conscious choice.
When we model what we do we need
to hear our conscience's voice.
For when we say, it's ok they're
not watching what we do,
We fool ourselves, they see it
all. It's up to me and you.

Speaks for itself, they're watching.

The Gnome of Clutter

There is a sneaky gnome that we all
know, that causes us to mutter.
What he looks like no one knows.
He's called the Gnome of Clutter.
He balls up socks and piles up clothes
right beneath our very nose.
When we wonder, "Who did this", no
one ever knows. The answer always
seems to be the same old," It's not me."
But there's a simple answer
to this age old mystery.
There seems to be one present,
in everybody's home.
The cause of all our clutter is
a guilty little gnome.

About the mysterious clutter that seems to
appear magically in all our lives.

Tears

Its only water, so they say, but I really wonder why. It's like a hammer in my breast when I see a tear in your eye. No feat of will, nor strength of arm can make it go away. A thing so soft has such power and that is why I say, "A tear in your eye is like a dagger in my heart."

This is about the difficulty of seeing someone's pain. Especially for men, who tend to feel powerless when women cry.

Masters of Darkness

I do not hear the darkness.
I move without hesitation in the
world of the owl and the bat.
Where others stumble and lose their nerve,
I slide through the inky blackness like a fog.
I see what the evil cannot, and go where
they don't dare, to do my work for freedom.
A navy seal does not fear the
blackness of night, he rules it.

A tribute to the US Navy Seals

El Tigre

He moves through the jungle
silently as if he weren't there.
His blazing eyes search the night
for the wary, who know he comes.
The chase is not fair and he is happy
to seek out the old, the sick and the young.
Sometimes he is successful, sometimes not.
Hunger is a frequent visitor to his being.
They are not strangers.
He is the lord of the night,
but, nature's rules govern him too.
The jaguar is perfect, as God made him,
the spirit of the jungle, El Tigre.

I wrote this for the fun of describing a
mysterious creature of the night.

Thadeus and Mouse/ Surprise Party

One day Deborah, the otter called on
Thadeus and Mouse. "Come with me
and I'll show you my house." They
both agreed with great delight. Surely
it would be an awesome sight.
Deborah scampered ahead, unable
to contain her joy. Thadeus strolled
along. He was in on the hidden ploy.
They came upon Lindsay the bright
unicorn, and Kyle the fleet winged horse,
and they both came along of, course.
Soon the house appeared. It had a neat
mud slide, but they were so surprised by
what they saw inside. Mouse was really
stunned. She could not believe her eyes.
All her friends were in the house, under a
banner that said "Happy Birthday Mouse."
Nancy the hummingbird fluttered happily
above the din as all Mouse' friends began
to wonder in. Cathie the honey bear and
Debbie the owl brought in a cake that

was quite a surprise. The frosting had
mushrooms and no candles, but fireflies.
Lorraine the chipmunk gave Mouse a
book. Joce and Duke brought cashews
to cook. Karen the cat brought a pretty
pink sweater and the Labradors brought
music to make the party better.
Mouse' brother Ron got more than one
glance as Greta the gazelle tried to
teach him to dance. The deer named
Nancy, who is quite a poet, told him
it was easy, he just didn't know it.

Along came Christin, the little red fox,
with a comb for Mouse's locks. Patrick
the polar bear brought plenty of ice
to cool down the punch made with
sugar and spice. Mallory the cocker
spaniel brought Brad the badger and
they joined Jimmie the groundhog
to give Mouse a special song.
Jell-O that floated in the air made
a desert beyond compare.
All sang and danced and had great
fun, with lots to eat for everyone.
Thadeus ate more than he should, and
wouldn't dance, even if he could.
Mouse laughed and danced with
every friend, until the party came
to an end. She said goodbye with

tears in her eyes and said "Thank you Thadeus, for a sweet surprise!

This is an example of my stories for children in which all the characters are friends and relatives in animal form, and there are no laws of nature.

Index

Edwards Brothers Malloy
Thorofare, NJ USA
June 2, 2016